Pablo Picasso

by Linda Lowery
illustrations by Janice Lee Porter

Carolrhoda Books, Inc./Minneapolis

For Judith Fisher—like Picasso, she has made her life a colorful expression of personal freedom.   *—L.L.*

For my dad—who showed me the artists, made art in his spare time, bought the art supplies, displayed the pictures, and sent me to art school—eternal love.   *—J.L.P.*

Text copyright © 1999 by Linda Lowery
Illustrations copyright © 1999 by Janice Lee Porter

Photographs courtesy of: © Corbis, pp. 30–31; Illustrated London News Picture Library, p. 46.

Publisher's note: The artwork in this book is inspired by the life and work of Pablo Picasso. Every effort was made to secure permission from the Picasso Administration to include reproductions of original Picasso paintings, but permission was denied.

This book is available in two editions:
Library binding by Carolrhoda Books, Inc.
Soft cover by First Avenue Editions
Divisions of the Lerner Publishing Group
241 First Avenue North, Minneapolis, MN 55401 U.S.A.

Website address: www.lernerbooks.com

Library of Congress Cataloging-in-Publication Data

Lowery, Linda.
    Pablo Picasso / by Linda Lowery ; illustrations by Janice Lee Porter.
      p. cm. — (Carolrhoda on my own books)
    Summary: Tells the story of Pablo Picasso as he grows through his early days as an artist, his discovery of cubism, and his later years of sculpture and painting to become a famous artist.
    ISBN 1–57505–331–4 (lib.bdg.) ISBN 1–57505–370–5 (pbk.)
    1. Picasso, Pablo, 1881–1973—Juvenile literature. 2. Artists—France—Biography—Juvenile literature. [1. Picasso, Pablo, 1881–1973. 2. Artists.] I. Porter, Janice Lee, ill. II. Title. III. Series.
N6853.P5L78 1999
709'.2—dc21
[B]
                                           99-21965

Manufactured in the United States of America
1 2 3 4 5 6 – JR – 04 03 02 01 00 99

Author's Note

When we look at a painting by Pablo Picasso, we each see it in a different way. I might see a beautiful woman, while you might see a jumble of puzzle pieces.

This is also true of the events that happened during Picasso's life. Everyone who knew him saw him in a different way. The stories they tell about him are all a little different. Pablo himself liked to brag and exaggerate. So we don't know exactly which facts about Picasso's life are entirely true.

We *do* know the facts about Picasso's art, however. And the art that Pablo Picasso created will always be the most exciting and most colorful part of his life.

Pablo Picasso stared at his math test.

He was confused.

Adding numbers made his mind go fuzzy.

It was 1891, and Pablo was nine.

When he looked at numbers,

all he saw were shapes and pictures.

"I'll show them what I can do!" he thought.

In his mind, he turned the numbers

into a beautiful pigeon.

4

The 0 looked like the pigeon's eye.

The 6 was its head and body.

The 3 fit perfectly under that,

making little bird feet.

The 2s became wings.

The line above the answer

looked just like a table

for the bird to perch its feet on!

And right under the pigeon's table

sat the answer: 13.

As a grown man, Pablo Picasso
told the pigeon story many times.
He loved to brag about his early days
as an artist.
The first word he ever said was *piz*,
which is short for "pencil" in Spanish.

His dark eyes flashed
when he told stories about his life
and his art.
Pablo was short, and his hands were small.
But his stories made him seem
gigantic and powerful.
So did his art.

As a young student, Pablo filled the margins
of his books with doodles.

He turned ink blobs into animals.

His teachers were not pleased.

They sent him to the "cells."
The cells were tiny rooms
of empty white walls
with nothing in them except a bench.
Most students hated to be all alone in a cell.
Not Pablo.
He took his pad of paper
and his pencil with him.
"I could have stayed there forever," he said,
"drawing, drawing, drawing."

Pablo's family lived in Spain.

Until he was 10, he lived

in the sunny south.

He drew what he saw around him:

people, pigeons, bullfights, and guitars.

When he went out to play,

he drew in the dirt with a stick.

At the seashore, he drew huge

dolphins in the sand.

At home, Pablo drew his little sister Lola.

Then Pablo's family moved to Corunna,
a rainy town on the Atlantic Ocean.
He made pictures of the lighthouse
and the foggy sea.
Pablo's father, Don José, was a painter.
He saw that his son was very talented.

When Pablo was 13,
his father asked him to finish a painting
he had started.
It was a picture of pigeons.

Pablo added the feet to his father's painting,

using his father's paints.

Pablo did such a wonderful job that

Don José gathered all his brushes and

paints and gave them to Pablo.

Pablo was excited.

He could finally work on real canvas

with real paints.

He painted beautiful portraits of people.

Pablo wanted to make money

from his paintings.

He carried his portraits to a junk shop

near his house.

The shopkeeper hung them

in the front window.

It was Pablo's first art show.

Two of his paintings were sold.

At 16, Pablo was too restless
to stay home.
He tried going to art school.
But it did not give him
the excitement he craved.
He moved to France.
Sometimes he went back to Spain
for long visits looking for adventure.
His art became adventurous, too.
Pablo had huge emotions—as big as
the stories he told about himself.
When he was mad, he was fiery.
When he was sad, he was stormy.
When he was happy, he was wildly joyful.
So why not put all those huge feelings
into his art?

When Pablo Picasso left home,

he had little money and often felt lonely.

He painted people who felt like he did:

homeless people and beggars and prisoners.

He did not paint them exactly

the way they looked in real life.

He made their faces and fingers

very long and droopy.

Mostly, he used blue paint,

even for the color of their skin.

This time is called Pablo Picasso's

"Blue Period."

Many of his Blue Period paintings

make people feel sad and lonely.

While making these sad paintings,

Pablo learned something about himself.

He needed people.

He liked to be alone to paint all day,

but he wanted to be with friends at night.

During his Blue Period, Pablo spent

some time in Barcelona, Spain.

But in 1904, he moved to Paris, France,

to a neighborhood called Montmartre.

It was full of artists.

Pablo met many friends there.

He also fell in love with a woman

named Fernande.

As he began to cheer up, he painted

some happier pictures.

He added pink and rosy colors

to his paintings.

This is called his "Rose Period."
But Pablo quickly got bored
with his happy paintings.

Pablo was like the weather—
changing all the time.
In 1907, he and his friend Georges
Braque tried out a new idea.
They painted things
that looked broken.
If they painted a cup, it looked
as if they had smashed the cup
against the wall.
Then they painted the broken pieces
all mixed up.
Some people had a hard time seeing
what was really in these paintings.
They could see only triangles,
squares, and cubes.
This new style was named "cubism."

Pablo was excited about cubism.

Every day, he worked and worked.

He made one cubist painting after the next.

Every night, Pablo and Georges
visited each other's studios.

"Each of us *had* to see what the other
had done during the day," Pablo said.

At first, most people thought
cubism was strange.
All over the world, people complained
about Picasso's new "broken" way
of painting.
Even Pablo's artist friends did not like
what he was doing.

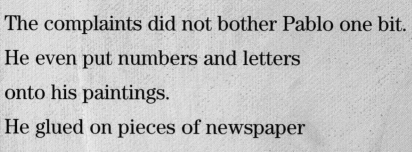

The complaints did not bother Pablo one bit.
He even put numbers and letters
onto his paintings.
He glued on pieces of newspaper
and sheet music.
He made a guitar out of cardboard, paper,
a tin can, and some wire.
Pablo was having lots of fun.
He and Georges started to wear
matching overalls when they painted.

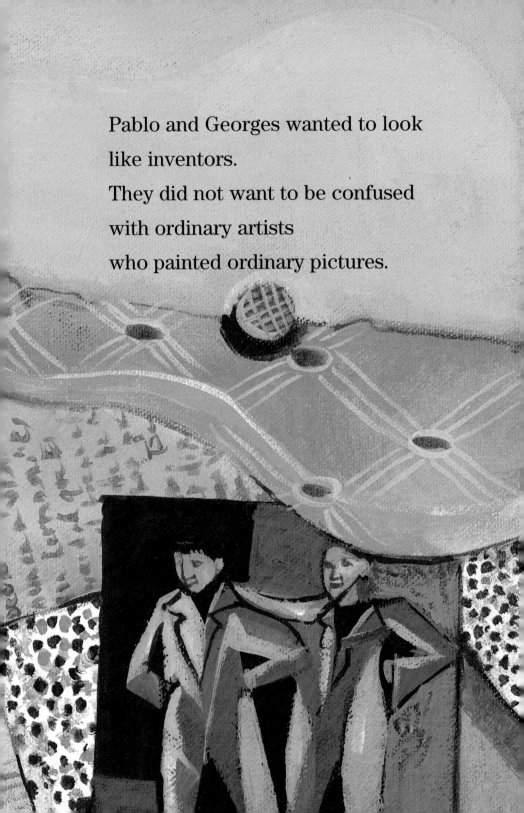

Pablo and Georges wanted to look
like inventors.
They did not want to be confused
with ordinary artists
who painted ordinary pictures.

As the years went on,

Pablo kept "drawing, drawing, drawing."

His art kept changing with his moods.

In 1936, war broke out in Spain.

Nazis from the German air force

flew warplanes over a Spanish town

called Guernica.

They destroyed the town with bombs

and killed 1,600 people.

Pablo got the news in Paris.

Rage tore through him.

Guernica was not far from Corunna,

where he had grown up.

How dare the Nazis destroy

the Spain he loved!

How dare they kill people

who had done nothing wrong!

What could he do?

Pablo Picasso fought back.

His weapons were not guns and bombs.

His weapons were pencils
and paintbrushes.

Pablo Picasso stretched a giant canvas.

It was 12 feet high and 26 feet long.

Only a huge space
would have room for his anger.

He painted horses and
people in flames.
He painted a child dead
in its mother's arms.
He painted women screaming,
with their heads thrown back
so heaven could hear their cries.
He painted their pain.
He painted his rage.
Pablo used no color in his picture—
no yellow, no red, no blue.
It was simply black and white and gray.

The painting was called *Guernica*,
after the town the Nazis had destroyed.
It gave Pablo some peace to know
he had told the terrible story of Guernica
through his painting.

Guernica *(1937)*
by Pablo Picasso

He could not change what
the Nazis had done.
But he had shown
everyone the truth.
Maybe that would help stop war from
happening in the world again.
In 1944, *Guernica* was put on display at the
World's Fair in Paris.
War was still going on in France then.

The Nazis hated *Guernica*.

One day, they came to see Pablo
in his studio.

They saw a photograph of *Guernica*.

"Did you do this?" one of them
asked Picasso.

Pablo's black eyes flashed.

He stood firm, his feet planted
on the floor of his studio.

"No," answered Pablo. "You did."

Pablo had not created the violence.

He had painted a picture that showed
how violent the Nazis were.

During the war, Pablo fell in love
with a woman named Françoise.
Pablo was 62, but he did not feel old.
He became the father of two children,
Claude and Paloma.
The family moved to southern France.

Pablo continued to create art—
even from trash!
Years before, he had found a seat
and handlebars from an old bike.
To him, they looked like a bull.
The seat was the head.
The handlebars were the horns.
He put them together and made a sculpture.

Every day, Pablo and Françoise
walked together to his studio.
As they walked, Pablo looked in trash cans
for treasures to take to his studio.
He turned a faucet and an old shovel
into a crane.
A wastebasket, tree branches,
and flowerpots became a goat.

He used two of Claude's toy cars
to make a baboon.
The cars made the head.
The ears were handles
from a broken pitcher.

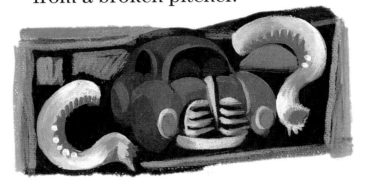

Claude was not very happy.
But Pablo was delighted.
He also made pottery:
vases, cups, and bowls.
He painted bullfights on plates
that he had made himself.
He scratched pictures in metal.
These were called engravings.

Pablo had become very famous.

Crowds of people often gathered outside

Pablo's studio, wanting to meet him.

If he was in a bad mood, he would

lock his doors and stay in bed.

"I live like a prisoner," he complained

when he was cranky.

If he was in a good mood,

he would let people visit.

He would tell them lively stories

about himself.

Pablo was proud to live his life
in his own way.
Sometimes he painted in his boxer shorts.
Other times, he wore colorful costumes
such as clown noses and gorilla feet,
cowboy hats and witch masks.
At night, he stayed up late with friends.
He told stories, argued about art,
and laughed until tears ran down his face.

Pablo Picasso was not easy to live with.
He was stubborn and bossy.
He did whatever pleased him,
even if it hurt the people he loved.
Finally, Françoise and Claude
and Paloma left.
Pablo found new people to love.
In 1961, he got married again, this time
to a woman named Jacqueline.

They often went to bullfights in Spain.
There, Pablo was the center of attention.
People shouted to him, calling him
"the best painter in the world."
Police guarded him from crowds of fans.
Bullfighters gave him gifts.
Sometimes they tossed him
a bullfighter's hat.

When Pablo was 85 years old,
the city of Chicago asked him to make
a sculpture for a building there.
He decided to make the sculpture
out of steel.
He drew the design.
But it was too big for him to build
by himself.
It was larger than anything
he had ever made.
It took 20 workers one year to cut the steel
and put up the sculpture.
Crowds and marching bands gathered
when it was finished.
When the cover was pulled off,
people did not know what to think.
Some people loved it.
Others said it looked like a rusty old dog.

Pablo refused to explain his sculpture.
He wanted people to imagine
whatever they saw in it.

Pablo believed art was magical.

When he drew and painted,

he did not think.

He let his mind wander

and his feelings run free.

"Everyone wants to understand art,"

Pablo complained.

He said art was like the song of a bird.

Why try to understand it?

To think about it too much

spoils the magic of the art.

All his life, Pablo never knew
what would happen when
he picked up a pencil or a paintbrush.
Each new creation seemed to appear
magically on the canvas.
People never knew what he would do next.
They were always surprised
by what they saw.
So was Pablo Picasso.

Pablo Picasso works on a painting in 1945.

Afterword

Pablo Picasso kept "drawing, drawing, drawing" until he died at age 91. Almost every day, from the time he was 13, Picasso drew in his journal and painted in his studio. He even painted until dawn the night before he died. He left behind 78 years of artwork.

Many of Picasso's works are very famous. Others can be hard to recognize. He was always trying new styles and new techniques—more than any artist who ever lived. There are Picasso plates and sculptures, Picasso paintings and collages, and Picasso engravings and drawings.

His work changed as he did, so Pablo Picasso's art always stayed new and young. Even in his old age, people called him "the youngest artist in the world."

Important Dates

October 25, 1881—Pablo Picasso was born in
  Málaga, Spain.
1894—Showed his paintings for first time in a
  Corunna junk shop
1895—Family settled in Barcelona, and Picasso
  entered Fine Arts Academy
1901—Began his Blue Period
1904—Moved to Paris, met Fernande Olivier, and
  began his Rose Period
1907—Began cubism
1937—Town of Guernica, Spain, destroyed; Picasso
  painted *Guernica*
1943—Met Françoise Gilot in Paris
1947—Claude born
1948—Took first of many trips to World Peace Congress
  meetings
1949—Paloma born
1961—Married Jacqueline Roque
1967—Chicago Monument finished
April 8, 1973—Died at Mougins, France, at age 91

AAX -6963